HOW IT WAS

CAVALIERS AND ROUNDHEADS

Stewart Ross

B. T. Batsford Ltd, London

CONTENTS

© Stewart Ross 1994

First published 1994

Typeset by Goodfellow & Egan Ltd, Cambridge

Printed in Hong Kong

Published by
B. T. Batsford Ltd
4 Fitzhardinge Street
London W1H 0AH

A CIP catalogue record for this book is available from the British Library.

ISBN 0 7134 7438 6

Cover illustration: *The fall of York, the king's capital in the north, to the Roundheads in July 1644. From a painting by Ernest Crofts (1847–1911).*

Frontispiece: Whitehall, January 30th, 1649 *by Ernest Crofts, showing the execution of Charles I.*

INTRODUCTION

During the first half of the seventeenth century it was not always clear how monarch and parliament should work together. Under the first two Stuart kings – James I and Charles I – this relationship came under increasing strain. James handled the situation better than his son Charles, who in 1629 decided to govern without calling parliament. This plan collapsed in the late 1630s when Charles and his archbishop, William Laud, tried to bring the church in Scotland more into line with that in England. The Scots rebelled, and the majority of the English political nation (the people with political power) refused to assist their king. Charles was therefore obliged to call an English parliament to raise funds. King and parliament were soon at loggerheads. Mistrust grew, and shrill voices of religious and political radicalism arose. Ireland rebelled. The English nation divided in three: Royalists (or Cavaliers), Parliamentarians (or Roundheads) and neutrals (the largest group). By the autumn of 1642 the Royalists and Parliamentarians were at war.

The fighting was sporadic and scattered, but nevertheless bitterly brutal. It lasted until early 1646, by which time the king had clearly lost the war. Yet the bloodshed settled nothing. After three years of hopeless negotiation and further fighting, the Parliamentary leaders had had enough. Giving up hope of ever reaching a settlement with Charles, in January 1649 they had him executed.

During the eleven-year Interregnum (time between reigns) Britain was a republic. First came a Commonwealth, governed by the remnants (the 'Rump') of Charles I's last parliament. Then came a Protectorate under Lord Protector Oliver Cromwell, the most forceful and successful Parliamentary general. He organized reform at home and enjoyed military success abroad. But the new regime rested on the army and the shoulders of the Lord Protector, and there was no clear plan for the future. A growing number of the political nation began to consider a restoration of the monarchy. When Cromwell died in September 1658, many people believed that if they did not bring back Charles I's elder son (Charles II) there would be more bloodshed and chaos. Thus in May 1660 Charles II landed at Dover, and was later crowned in London. The politics of the early years of his reign, when as far as possible past differences were forgotten and an attempt was made to put the clock back to where it had been before the Civil War, are called the Restoration.

Behind this apparently simple tale of a rebellion that failed lie some of the most significant themes in British history: How should the three kingdoms of England, Ireland and Scotland relate to each other? What should be the faith and organization of the Church of England? And, most basic of all, what should be the balance of power between king and parliament? The Civil War, Interregnum and Restoration were the first three acts of a five act play. In 1688 Charles II's brother, King James II, was expelled from the kingdom. This was the beginning of a settlement known as the Glorious Revolution (1688–1701), which is still part of the British constitution.

So who were the Cavaliers and Roundheads and what were they really fighting about? Why did the Roundheads win the war? Why was there no settlement with Charles I? What did ordinary people think about what was happening? What part did religion play in shaping events? Why did the Interregnum fail to survive? What was restored on Charles II's return to power? This book will help you to answer these and other questions. In so doing it will open a window onto the most exciting and important period in British history.

Introductory quiz

Do you know?

Why were the Parliamentarians called 'Roundheads'?

Which was the first battle of the Civil War?

What happened at Whitehall on 30 January 1649?

What happened to Christmas during the Interregnum?

What did the Act of Indemnity and Oblivion say?

KING CHARLES I

In the seventeenth century government was a very personal matter. Monarchs were expected to rule as well as reign. They were not just the figurehead of the nation, but the Supreme Governor of the Church of England and responsible for day-to-day administration. In theory they made all important appointments, took all important decisions and conducted relations with foreign powers. To help them they had such ministers and civil servants as they could afford. When they wished to call one, they also had a parliament representing the most powerful members of society. Calling parliament was a useful way of finding out the mood of the country. If that mood was favourable, members of the House of Commons and House of Lords could vote the king large sums of money. He needed this because his income from lands and other sources, such as customs, was not enough. But if he mishandled parliament, particularly the House of Commons, it could quickly turn nasty.

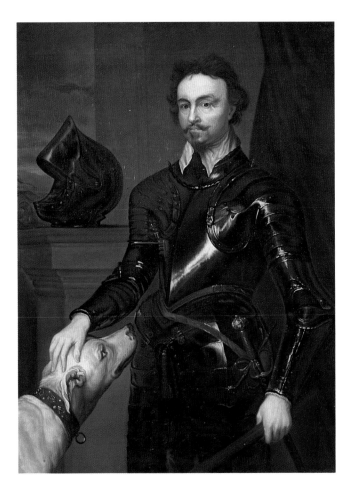

James I (1603–25), who came to the throne on the death of his cousin Queen Elizabeth I, was an intelligent but eccentric man. He had been king of Scotland long before he came to the English throne (which is why he is also referred to as James VI). Using this experience, he managed to govern the whole of the British Isles – a near-impossible task – remarkably well. While he did not manage England's relations with the major European countries so effectively and ran up huge debts, at his death in 1625 his kingdoms were in reasonably good order. Unfortunately, his son inherited neither his father's ability to get on with people nor his political skill.

King Charles I (1625–49) was a short, sensitive, deeply religious man with a stammer. He was brave and had an excellent eye for beautiful works of art, but these could not make him a successful ruler. In early life he was overshadowed by his talented and more attractive brother and sister. When he grew up, he was not good at assessing situations or personalities, and he sometimes hid his self-doubt by being annoyingly obstinate. On other occasions he gave way easily, agreeing to radical changes of policy. Few people felt they knew where they were with him, and he was impossible to negotiate with.

The first five years of Charles' reign did not go well. Under the king's inexperienced leadership the country went to war with Spain (1625) and France (1627). The Duke of Buckingham, Charles' unpopular favourite, led expensive military expeditions against the Spanish port of Cadiz and the French island of Rhé. Both ventures failed. Three parliaments were called, each more critical of royal policy and management than the last. The third passed the famous Petition of Right (1628) against arbitrary (not bound by law or custom) government. Charles' tactless behaviour made things more difficult. He seemed to favour a new religious movement, *Arminianism* (see Glossary), which denied one or two of the Church of England's traditional teachings and favoured religious ceremony. Some anxious Protestants feared this was a step towards hated Roman Catholicism. The king also imprisoned without trial those who refused to lend him money.

Buckingham was assassinated in 1628. The following year a handful of hot-tempered MPs refused to leave the House of Commons until they

(Above) *George Villiers, the powerful favourite of both James I and Charles I. He became, in succession, Master of the Horse, Knight of the Garter, Earl of Buckingham. Master of the Wardrobe, Marquis of Buckingham, Lord High Admiral and, finally, Duke of Buckingham in 1623.*

(Left) *Charles on horseback, painted by Anthony van Dyck in 1638. Although small, the king was an able horseman and a brave soldier.*

(Far left) *In the first years of Charles I's reign Thomas Wentworth opposed the government in parliament. However, in 1628 he was made President of the Council of the North and rapidly rose to become one of the most powerful and feared men in the kingdom.*

had passed three resolutions against Arminianism and taxes raised without parliament's approval. The king arrested them and decided that in future he would manage without parliament.

Those who look favourably on what Charles and his ministers were trying to do in the period that followed (1629–40) call it the Personal Rule. But to opponents it was an Eleven Years' Tyranny. To begin with it seemed harmonious enough. Peace was made with France and Spain. The government managed its finances satisfactorily and urged local government officers to take their tasks more seriously. In Ireland, the king's Deputy Thomas Wentworth, Earl of Strafford (probably his most able minister), had some success in getting the king's command obeyed in that troubled island.

But the Personal Rule did not last. In the end it was brought down not by events in England or Ireland, but by Charles' unwise religious policy towards Scotland.

The Divine Right of Kings

During the 1620s England was not a country on the brink of civil war. At the time such a conflict was inconceivable. Nevertheless, the tensions between the king and some of his subjects raised fundamental questions which, in the end, they could not settle without fighting. The central issue was the power of the crown. While admitting he would be foolish to misuse his authority, James I had been quite clear just how great his power was. It came directly from God – the Divine Right of Kings.

> The state of monarchy is the supremest thing upon earth; for kings are not only God's lieutenants upon earth, and sit upon God's throne, but even by God himself they are called Gods.
>
> (Speech to parliament, 21 March 1610, cited in Kenyon, J., *The Stuart Constitution*, 1966)

Popish soap

Charles annoyed many people by using his royal prerogative (power) to grant monopolies. A monopoly was the exclusive right to do or make something. The king said that monopolies protected the public. In fact, they were usually a way of raising money, because the wealthy often bought monopolies from the king. One unwelcome monopoly was the right to make soap. The new soap was doubly unpopular because (1) it burned the hands of those who used it and (2) the monopolists who profited by it were thought to be Roman Catholic.

> Whereas ... persons under no government have made bad and unserviceable soap ... in secret and obscure places ... to the great ... damage of our loving subjects ... We ... for the prevention of the said ... abuses ... have thought fit by the advice of our Privy Councillors to incorporate into one body ... persons ... such as have been exercised and trained up in the ... trade of making soap.
>
> (Patent Rolls, 13 Car. I, xxxix)

Q

If James believed kings were answerable only to God, why do you think he thought they should govern wisely?

CHECK YOUR UNDERSTANDING

Can you remember the meaning of the following:

Ship Money
assize
Divine Right of Kings
tyranny
constitution

A somewhat fanciful engraving of Charles I on the throne in the House of Lords. (It was against tradition for kings to enter the Commons.)

CAN YOU REMEMBER ?

What was the name of Charles I's favourite?
When was Charles' Personal Rule?
What famous petition did the king accept in 1628?
Who was Lord Deputy in Ireland for most of the 1630s?
Who was the Supreme Governor of the Church of England?

Unpopular Ship Money

The king's government was quite active during Charles' Personal Rule, 1629–40. Royal interference in parish and county matters was resented by local officers, such as magistrates, sheriffs and constables. The issue that most irritated them was Ship Money, a tax to pay for the upkeep of the navy. It was not a new tax, but because it raised more than a grant from parliament, Charles tried to levy it more regularly and thoroughly than before. In particular, he asked counties that had no coastline to pay. By 1639, at the height of the Scottish rebellion, income from Ship Money had fallen away drastically because of a tax strike.

At the assizes [trials] at Maidstone, [when] Judge Weston . . . came to speak of ship-money, the audience – which had before hearkened [listened] but with ordinary attention – did then . . . listen with great diligence. After the declaration [had been] made I did . . . see a kind of dejection in their very looks . . .

(Memorandum in the papers of Sir Roger Twysden, a Kent magistrate, in K. Fincham, ed., *The Bulletin of the Institute of Historical Research*, vol. LVII, no. 136, 1984. Punctuation simplified)

Note in this extract the king is using a judge to deal with a political matter.

Q

Why do you think there was a 'dejection' in people's looks when they heard about Ship Money?

A page from the Parish Book of Great Kimble in Buckinghamshire, listing the landowners who refused to pay Ship Money in January 1635.

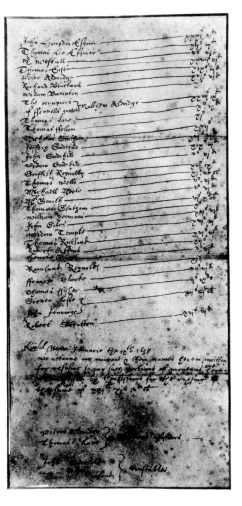

THINGS TO DO

1 Imagine you are one of those signing the Great Kimble Parish book of Buckinghamshire. Write a letter to the sheriff explaining why you do not think the Ship Money is fair.

2 Charles angered many people by granting monopolies – that is, allowing one group of people the sole right to do or make something without fear of competition. Next time you play Monopoly, the popular boardgame, try to work out how it got its name.

Plain Copy of Record of Meeting.

	s.	d.
John Hampden, Esquier	31	6
Thomas Lee, Esquier	41	3
Mrs. Westall	5	6
Thomas East	27	6
Peter Aldridge	19	3
Richard Blackwell	16	6
Widow Bampton	10	0
The Occupiers of flenell's Grove }Matthew Aldridge	24	9
Thomas Lane	10	9
Thomas ffellow	11	0
Nicholas Statham	22	0
Jeffery Goodchild	16	6
John Goodchild	19	3
Widow Goodchild	5	6
Griffith Reynolds	13	9
Thomas Wells	11	5½
Micheal Neele	5	6
M. Smith	5	6
Thomas Statham	6	10½
William Yeoman	16	6
John Giles	16	6
Widow Temple	16	6
Thomas Rutland	16	6
Robert Atkins	12	0
Henrie Short	5	6
Rowland Reynolds	11	6
ffrancis Clarke	7	6
Thomas ffisher	2	9
Steven Lasie }	12	4½
John Jennings }		
Robert Stratton	16	6

Kimbell Magna, Januarie the 9th, 1635.
We returne our warrant of their names herein written, for refusing to pay such portions of money as are herewithin assessed by the Assessours for the raysing of the sume of £21. 11s. 5½d.

PETER ALDRIDGE, } Assessours.
THOMAS LANE,

JOHN GOODCHILD, } Constables.
THOMAS RUTLAND,

ARCHBISHOP WILLIAM LAUD

For most of the seventeenth century, the Christian religion, as set out by the Church of England, was the foundation of society. With science in its infancy, religion explained the mysteries of the universe. The church's rituals gave a shape and pattern to daily life. Its teachings offered a code of conduct for people to live by. Furthermore, the church provided the king with a ready-made network of communication and control. Everyone was expected to belong to the Church of England and everyone was expected to go to church.

The Church of England, or Anglican church, was a moderate Protestant institution. It was first set up by Henry VIII (1509–47), then re-established by Elizabeth I (1558–1603). Unlike many other Protestant churches, it kept some aspects of Roman Catholicism, such as bishops. At first this compromise (half-way) position irritated both Roman Catholics and puritans. *Puritans* – described by a contemporary as the 'hotter sort of Protestants' – were enthusiasts who wished the church 'purified' of all remains of Popery (Catholicism). They wanted plain church buildings, simple services, holy Sundays and plenty of Bible study and sermons. However, after more than sixty years of careful control by Elizabeth and James, the tension between the puritans and the Anglicans had largely died down. The Church of England had begun to find a place in the hearts and minds of the people. Nevertheless, there were potential trouble spots.

The Scottish church (the *Kirk*) was more firmly and proudly Protestant than the Church of England. It took less notice of royal authority, too. The majority of the Irish were Roman Catholic who disliked the Protestant church. Many English had an intense, illogical fear of Catholicism. This had been built up by events such as the Spanish Armada (1588) and the Gunpowder Plot (1605) and by stories of Catholic atrocities during the religious wars raging on the Continent since 1618. Finally, as James I found in 1618 when he failed to get his *Book of Sports* (suggested useful pursuits for Sundays) accepted, the puritans could still be difficult. All these situations required very tactful handling.

William Laud became Charles' archbishop of Canterbury in 1633. Earnest, red-faced, humourless

and energetic he was not a tactful man. He and Wentworth, adopting the watchword 'thorough', were the key figures in the king's non-parliamentary government. In his quest for order, uniformity and reform Laud once wrote to the Lord Deputy, 'Thorough let us go, and spare not!' Such an attitude was hardly likely to produce religious harmony.

Charles and Laud wanted more control of the Church of England. Unlike James I, they were not prepared to turn a blind eye. If they did not like what they saw, they tried to do something about it. They wanted neat churchyards, priests in surplices,

(Left) The Trance and Vision of William Laud, *a contemporary engraving showing all the 'miserable cruelties and unheard of tyrannies caused by popish factions' witnessed by Archbishop Laud (Figure 'A') in his dream. Can you recognize which figure is Charles I?*

A portrait of William Laud painted about 1636.

altars railed off at the eastern end of churches and services accompanied by a moderate degree of ceremony. All preachers had to be licensed. To many puritans all this looked like a revolution – an Arminian revolution, or, worse, a Popish revolution.

Charles knew little of Scotland, Laud knew even less. As a result, many Scots believed their rulers cared little about them, particularly on matters of religion. Matters came to a head in 1637–8. Trying to bring the Kirk more into line with the Church of England, and without consulting a Scottish parliament or religious Assembly, Charles ordered the Kirk to accept new Canons (church regulations) and to use a new prayer book. When the prayer book was first used, Edinburgh exploded into riot. The Scots organized a National Covenant and called an illegal Assembly, which split up the Kirk. Charles determined to fight, although he had neither army, money nor support. The Bishops' Wars of 1639 and 1640 led to his total humiliation. The 'small cloud in the north' was not blown away. By June 1640 Scottish rebels had occupied the north of England. In the Treaty of Ripon, signed in June, Charles agreed to pay the Scots £300,000. That meant summoning an English parliament.

The Puritan reaction

This is the sort of response Laud's behaviour evoked from the puritans:

> Now I beseech you look upon the pride and ingratitude of . . . [the bishops]. What is it that this world can yield [give] to mortal creatures, that they possess not? Great and mighty are their privileges, and yet they are neither thankful to God nor the King . . .
>
> But how magnificent and glorious will [Laud] be . . . having . . . a great number of gentlemen . . . waiting on him; some of them carrying up his tail, for the better breaking and venting of his wind . . .
>
> (The Letany of John Bastwick, 1637)

Bearing in mind the date of this account, who do we have to be careful before accepting it at face value?

Not surprisingly, Bastwick was punished for such scurrilous (rude and insulting) writing. But the punishment he and his puritan colleagues Henry Burton and William Prynne received was so harsh that they became popular heroes. Prynne was branded with the initials S L – seditious libeller (telling lies to undermine the state).

> *June 30* The said three prisoners were brought to the New Palaceyard at Westminster to suffer according to their sentence . . . Mr. Burton spake much while in the pillory to the people: the executioner cut off his ears deep and close in a cruel manner with much effusion of blood, an artery being cut, as there was likewise of Dr Bastwick: then Mr. Prynne's cheeks were seared with an iron made exceeding hot, which done, the executioner cut off one of his ears and a piece of his cheek with it; then hacking the other ear almost off, he left it hanging and went down; but being called up again, he cut it quite off.
>
> (J. Rushworth, *Historical Collections*, 1659)

THINGS TO DO

1 Burton, Bastwick and Prynne were punished by the court of Star Chamber. From a book on Tudor history find out how this court got its name and what sort of reputation it had?

2 Find a church near you which was built before the religious reformation of the sixteenth century and see if you can discover what changes were made to it in the period 1530–1660.

Of God, Of Man, Of the Divell.

Dirty churchyards

Often it was not so much *what* Laud and Charles tried to do that annoyed people so much as *how* they tried to do it. For example, the new Scottish prayer book did not say anything particularly controversial, but what did annoy the Scots was that Charles issued it without consulting them first. This extract from Laud's orders to the Dean and Chapter of Worcester Cathedral gives some idea of his abrupt, unfriendly manner.

> 2. Item, that none be admitted into . . . your choir before he be first approved of for his voice and skill in singing . . .
>
> 3. Item, that hoods, square caps and the surplice be constantly used . . . by . . . ministers . . . whenever they come to administer or hear divine service . . .
>
> 6. Item, that your churchyard be decently . . . kept, and that you take care . . . that the bones of the dead may not lie scattered up and down, but that they be gathered together and buried; and that the chapel . . . at the end of your cathedral, now . . . made a hay barn, be restored . . . to the wonted [proper] use.
>
> (Orders following Laud's visit of 1635 in W. Scott and J. Bliss, eds., *The Works of William Laud*, 1847–60)

Why do you think Laud was not happy at the way churchyards were being used?

A puritan woodcut attacking Laud's bishops. One holds the Bible, another the service book and the third, on the right, a book entitled 'superstition'. Do you think the artist is suggesting that bishops could not distinguish between the three?

Early morning prayers

All her life Anne Halkett, daughter of one of Charles I's tutors, was grateful to her mother for her religious upbringing. This passage is an interesting insight into the importance of religious faith in the seventeenth century. It also shows that it was not just the opponents of the Church of England who were deeply religious.

> My mother's greatest care . . . was the great care she took that even from our infancy we were instructed never to neglect to begin and end the day with prayer, and orderly every morning to read the Bible, and . . . to keep [go to] the church as often as there was . . . prayers or preaching . . . I was seldom absent from divine service at five o'clock in the morning in the summer and six o'clock in the winter, till the . . . [puritans] put a restraint to that . . . worship so long . . . continued in the Church of England.
>
> (From the *Memoirs* of Anne, Lady Halkett, written in the seventeenth century and first published in 1875)

Which part of this extract tells us that Lady Anne was an Anglican?

CAN YOU REMEMBER ?

What letters were branded on Prynne's cheeks?
Which treaty was signed in June 1640?
What book did King James issue in 1618?
What did Charles try to get the Scots to accept in 1637?
When did Laud become Archbishop of Canterbury?

CHECK YOUR UNDERSTANDING

Can you remember the meaning of the following:

Popery
Kirk
Anglican
puritan
libeller

JOHN PYM, MP

By late 1640 Charles I had a serious crisis on his hands. Earlier in the year he had called an English parliament (the Short Parliament), but dismissed it because its members were more interested in their own grievances (complaints) than in fighting the Scots. The royal campaign during the Second Bishops' War, ending in the Treaty of Ripon, was a disaster. Charles had to call another parliament (later known as the Long Parliament) to meet on 3 November, yet there was no talk of civil war. Indeed, war was impossible because there were not two sides capable of fighting. As Charles' failure to quash the Scottish revolt showed, he had virtually no support. The themes of the next twenty months are (1) how the king gradually built up a following and (2) how, through a series of blunders, chances and misunderstandings, Royalists and Parliamentarians drifted slowly into war.

John Pym first entered parliament in 1621. He had always sided with those making life difficult for the royal government, and he contacted the Scots when the Short Parliament failed. Soon after the meeting of the Long Parliament, it was clear that Pym – 'King Pym' as he was nicknamed – was the leader of the various groups in the House of Commons who opposed the government. Tough, a fine speaker, good with figures and a superb political tactician, Pym was the spokesman for dissenting MPs during the breakdown with the king and the drift to war. Before almost anyone else, he realized just how serious was the business which he and the other royal critics in parliament had begun. To the king such men were traitors, and Charles did not believe he had to negotiate or keep his word with them. Therefore, Pym knew there could be no turning back. If parliament were dissolved (dismissed) the opposition MPs would have to face the king's anger on their own.

The Long Parliament gathered amid an atmosphere of great excitement. More extreme puritans believed the Church of England would soon collapse and God would rule the earth in person. MPs and peers (members of the House of Lords) arranged for the Scots to be paid. They then condemned Charles' key minister Strafford to death by a Bill of Attainder (a law declaring him to be guilty). Charles signed the Bill and his most able ally was executed on 12 May 1641.

Next, the opposition MPs took steps to prevent Parliament being dissolved without their consent. They went on to get rid of the parts of the Personal Rule which they disliked most. These included Ship Money and the king's prerogative law courts such as the Star Chamber. So far the great majority of MPs had been in agreement. But they had not yet tackled the really thorny question – religion. In the summer of 1641, when this issue could be put off no longer, the first serious divisions among MPs began to appear.

Matters took a turn for the worse when, on a visit to Scotland, Charles was mixed up in an attempted coup (the Incident). At about the same time news started filtering in of a serious Catholic rebellion in Ireland. To put this down, the king required parliament to give him money for an army. But MPs feared he would use the soldiers against parliament, so no money was forthcoming. The situation grew more tense by the week. In November Pym organized the Grand Remonstrance, a list of all the complaints against the government under Charles I, which was addressed to the nation. On 4 January 1642, in an attempt to arrest the opposition ringleaders, Charles marched into the House of Commons with a troop of soldiers, but his intended victims had fled. The king left London and began a 'paper war', in which each side tried to win support by setting out its position in pamphlets and broadsheets. Finally, after all efforts at reaching an agreement had failed, on 22 August 1642 the king raised his standard on Nottingham Castle. The Civil War had begun.

The speaker of the House of Commons sets out MPs' traditional rights (free speech, freedom from arrest, etc.) when Charles I comes to arrest the five members in 1642.

The Grand Remonstrance

By the autumn of 1641 a growing number of MPs and peers were becoming alarmed at the way events were developing. Fearing that the whole fabric of church and state was under threat, they instinctively moved closer to the king. The vote on the Grand Remonstrance, which had been printed and circulated among the ordinary people, marked a significant turning point.

> We, your most humble and obedient subjects, do with all faithfulness and humility beseech your Majesty,
>
> 1. That you will be graciously pleased to concur [agree] with the humble desires of your people in a parliamentary way . . .
>
> For depriving the Bishops of their votes in Parliament, and abridging their immoderate power . . .
>
> 2. That your Majesty will likewise be pleased to remove from your council all such as . . . favour and promote any of those pressures and corruptions wherewith your people have been grieved . . .
>
> (From the Petition accompanying the Grand Remonstrance, presented to the king, 1 December 1641)

The Grand Remonstrance was radical (extreme) stuff and it was eventually passed by only eleven votes. There were now two clear sides to the conflict. Sir Edward Dering was worried.

> Mr Speaker, when I heard of a Remonstrance, I . . . imagined that like faithful councillors, we should hold up a glass [mirror] unto his Majesty: I thought to represent unto [show] the King the wicked counsels of pernicious councillors . . .
>
> I did not dream that we should remonstrate downward, tell stories to the people and talk of the King as of a third person.
>
> The use and end of such a Remonstrance I understand not . . .
>
> (J. Rushworth, *Historical Collections*, 1721)

Q

If the king had agreed to these requests, which of his powers would he have been giving away? What did Dering mean by 'tell stories to the people'?

THINGS TO DO

1 Imagine you are an MP in 1641. Decide whether you will vote for or against the Grand Remonstrance and its accompanying petition and write a letter home explaining your decision.

2 Suggest ways in which Charles might have defused the situation which had arisen by late 1641.

3 Using local histories in your public library, try and find out the name of the MPs for your district (there were borough and county MPs) at the time of Civil War. Did they side with King or Parliament?

CAN YOU REMEMBER ?

By what majority was the Grand Remonstrance passed?

Which Parliament first met on 3 November 1641?

Why could there have been no Civil War in 1640?

What did Charles I fail to do on 4 January 1642?

Where did the king raise his standard?

Who was executed on 12 May 1641?

CHECK YOUR UNDERSTANDING

Can you remember the meaning of the following:

Remonstrance
radical
a glass (in 17th century)
peers

Master PYM
HIS SPEECH
In *Parliament*, on *Wednesday*, the
fifth of *January*, 1641.

Concerning the Vote of the House of *Commons*,
for his discharge upon the Accusation of High
Treason, exhibited against himselfe, and the
Lord *Kimbolton*, Mr. *Iohn Hampden*, Sr.
Arthur Haslerig, Mr. *Strowd*,
M. Hollis, by his Maiesty.

The true Effigies of Mr. *Iohn Pym*, Esquire

London Printed for I. W, 1641.

John Pym speaking to parliament in 1641. More than anything else, it was his political skill that held together the diverse groups opposed to the royal government.

High Treason

The decision to attack Strafford almost as soon as the Long Parliament had met was a clever one. It united MPs and showed that they were critical of the king's ministers, not Charles himself. But all along Strafford had served the king to the best of his ability, so he was not an easy man to convict of treason. In the end, he was condemned guilty by Act of Parliament.

[The] words, counsels and actions of the ... Earl of Strafford were spoken ... by [him] ... traitorously, and contrary to his allegiance [duty] to our sovereign lord the King. [He wanted] ... to ... withdraw the hearts and affections of the King's ... people ... from his Majesty, and to set division between them, and to ruin and destroy his Majesty ...

(From the Articles against Strafford, January 1641)

Why do you think Charles I signed the Bill condemning Strafford to death?

A Woman's Fears

As the gap between King and Parliament widened, many people were frightened at what might happen. Lady Brilliana Harley, although delighted by parliament's attacks on Laud and his bishops, did not want war. A year after she wrote these words to her husband, her castle at Brampton Bryan was besieged by the king's forces. She died shortly after she had driven them off.

23 April, 1642 I am persuaded things are now come to their ripeness, and if God cannot be very merciful to us, we shall be in a distressed condition. Doctor Wright [a puritan] desires you ... buy him two muskets ... and fifteen or sixteen pounds of [gun]powder in a barrel.

29 April, 1642 I see the distance is still kept between the king and parliament. The Lord in his mercy make them one ...

(From *The Letters of Lady Brilliana Harley*, first published in 1854)

In this passage, what did Lady Harley mean by 'things are now come to their ripeness'?

CIVIL WAR

The English Civil War lasted for more than three years. To begin with the fighting was rather half-hearted and negotiations between king and Parliament continued on and off into 1643. Even well into the final year, with several armies battling up and down the kingdom, the outcome was not certain. However the *Royalists* (nicknamed *Cavaliers* by their enemies, meaning easy-going, rather undisciplined horsemen) were unable to win the one great victory they needed. The strength and efficiency of the *Parliamentarians* (nicknamed *Roundheads* after the close-cut hair worn by some of them) ground the Royalists down, and the fighting finally died out in the first few months of 1646.

Throughout the war Charles suffered from losing control of his capital, London. Not surprisingly, shortly after hostilities had begun he tried to get the city back. Marching south to Edgehill in Warwickshire, on 23 October 1642 he met a Roundhead army under the command of the Earl of Essex. Despite a dashing and successful cavalry charge by Prince Rupert, the one experienced general in the field, neither side won this first major battle. Nevertheless, Essex withdrew and the way lay open for the Royalists to march on London. By 13 November they were at the village of Turnham Green, only a few miles from their destination. It looked as if the war might end in Royalist victory

after only a few months. But the well armed and organized trained bands (local volunteers) of London turned out to defend their city. With winter drawing in, the king decided to retreat to Oxford, where he set up his headquarters.

The following year (1643) began well for Charles. In February his French queen, Henrietta Maria, arrived from France with arms and money. Then came victory at Chalgrove Field, near Oxford. The loyal Duke of Newcastle captured much of the north of England and Sir Ralph Hopton did the same in the south west with a victory at Roundway Down. But now Charles heard that Newcastle had been defeated at Gainsborough by the Eastern Association, a Parliamentarian army based in East Anglia. The Royalists also failed to take Gloucester. After a drawn battle at Newbury on 20 September – sometimes said to be the turning point of the war – the king was unable to continue his advance along the Thames valley towards London. Worse was to come.

Although Charles had freed troops for his English campaigns by signing a truce with the Irish rebels, at almost the same time Parliament won the support of the Scots. By an agreement known as the Solemn League and Covenant (promise), the Scottish rebels (Covenanters) undertook to give

Parliament military help. The value of this help became clear the following summer. On 2 July a Parliamentary army, including cavalry under the up-and-coming commander Oliver Cromwell, met Prince Rupert's Royalist army on Marston Moor in Yorkshire. The prince's army was destroyed. The north of England fell under Parliamentary control. Still Charles did not despair. The Royalist Earl of Montrose was winning a remarkable series of battles against the Covenanters in the Highlands of Scotland. The Royalists had further success in the south west, and there were signs of serious disagreement among the Parliamentary leaders.

As it turned out, Parliament's problems did not help the king. Instead, they led to the formation of a new, well funded, well organised military force called the New Model Army. Command went to Cromwell and Sir Thomas Fairfax, both dedicated to total defeat of the king. On 14 June 1645 the New Model Army utterly destroyed Charles' army at Naseby in Leicestershire. Further Royalist reverses followed at Langport and Rowton Heath. Bristol surrendered to Parliament on 10 September. Three days later Montrose was overcome at Philiphaugh. The king left his Oxford headquarters in disguise on 27 April 1646. On 5 May he surrendered to the Scots near Newark. He had lost the war.

(Left) Siege of Oxford *by Jan Wyck (1640–1702). Oxford was besieged by Parliamentary troops. The university city was the Royalist capital for 3½ years, the king holding court in Christ Church College. On the king's command it finally surrendered on 24 June 1646.*

(Right) Attack on the baggage train – Edgehill, *painted by Richard Beavis (1824–1896) The common soldier generally welcomed the chance of plunder to boost his meagre wages.*

CIVIL WAR

Fear and Misery

The horror of war did not come home to most English men and women until Edgehill, particularly during the frosty night after the conflict, when the screams and groans of the wounded rose into the clear, cold sky. But the slaughter at Naseby was worse:

> I saw the field so bestrewn with carcasses of horses and men, the bodies lay slain about four miles in length, but most thick on the hill where the king stood.
>
> (Written in 1645 and first published in E.G.B. Warburton, *Memoirs of Prince Rupert and the Cavaliers*, 1849)

The poet Edward Benlowes put his feelings in verse.

> Edgehill, with graves looked white
> With blood looked red
> Maz'd [amazed] at the numbers of the dead.
> (Canto XII)

King Charles' last great battle of the war: the opposing armies at Naseby, in which the New Model Army showed its clear superiority.

Why were the English so shocked by the horrors of war?

CAN YOU REMEMBER ?

When and to whom did Charles I give himself up?
How many men were killed in battle during the Civil Wars?
What title did Queen Henrietta Maria give herself?
Who was the most experienced commander in 1642?
In which battle did the Scots first give Parliament decisive support?
Which castle did Lady Harley defend so bravely?

CHECK YOUR UNDERSTANDING

Can you remember the meaning of the following:

New Model Army
trained bands
Covenanters
capital city
Cavaliers
Roundheads

THINGS TO DO

1 Research one of the major Civil War battles. Write an account of the fighting from the point of view of an ordinary foot soldier.
2 Mark in the major Civil War battles on an outline map of Britain.
3 Give your own reasons why you think the king was so desperate to capture London.

Women at War

Although women did not join in the hand-to-hand fighting on the battlefield, many of them played an important part in the war. Queen Henrietta Maria worked tirelessly for her husband, seeking help from abroad and marching about the countryside with an escort of 5000, calling herself 'She-Majesty Generalissima over all'. More often, women were caught up in garrison duty and sieges. Brilliana Harley successfully held Brampton Bryan during a seven-week assault.

Upon the 7th [August] in the afternoon . . . [the enemy] planted another great gun against the west part of our castle. The third shot the bullet came in at a window, shattered the walls, which hurt the Lady Colburn, struck out one of her eyes. Lieutenant-Colonel Wright's wife was hurt, but neither of them mortally . . . Upon the 9th the enemy planted five great guns, as if they meant this day to gave beaten it to dust. . . . The noble lady [Brilliana] was . . . more courageous than ever . . .

(Captain Priamus Davies, *An Account of the Siege of Brampton Bryan Castle*, written in the seventeenth century and first published in 1904)

The Most Bloody War

Civil wars are the worst kind of wars. They set brother against brother, children against parents, family against family, village against village. They are often the most bloody, too. There were some 635 different battles during the wars 1639–48 (a Second Civil War was fought in 1648). The nine major battles accounted for only about 15 per cent of casualties. The estimated casualty totals given below represent a considerably higher proportion of the population killed than in either the First or Second World Wars.

CASUALTIES		TAKEN PRISONER	
Killed in combat		Parliament	34,000
Parliament	34,000	Royalist	83,000
Royalist	51,000		
Total	85,000		
Died from disease etc.	100,000		
Killed by accidents	300		
Died in Bishops' Wars	500		
Total	186,800		

Note that these figures do not show the number of wounded – many soldiers remained crippled for life.
(These figures and those in the paragraph above are from Charles Carlton, 'The Impact of the Fighting', in John Morrill, ed., *The Impact of the English Civil War*, 1991)

Why do you think that more Cavaliers than Roundheads were killed in the Civil Wars?

The grisly fate of traitors – two men who attempted to betray the City of London are hanged by Parliamentary authorities.

CAVALIERS AND ROUNDHEADS

Today the names 'Cavalier' and 'Roundhead' conjure up clear and vivid images. We think of the Cavaliers as rather happy-go-lucky, jolly, outgoing people with long hair and bright clothes, and the Roundheads as earnest, sober and straightforward. This simple distinction is based more on folklore than historical fact. The two sides in the English Civil War were a very complex mix.

Historians used to think that the Royalists were largely members of the landed aristocracy (nobles) and their followers, while the Parliamentarians were people from lower down the social scale: the gentry, craftsmen and urban (town) workers. In other words, the Civil War was seen as a class war. There is some truth in this view. For example, the majority of peers fought for the king.

Prince Rupert, Charles I's nephew. Having fought in Germany before the outbreak of the English Civil War, in 1642 he was one of the few commanders on either side with any military experience.

Nevertheless, in general the two sides cut across social class, community and even family. Some great nobles, such as the Earls of Essex and Manchester, fought for Parliament. Sometimes, as in Kent in 1642, the sides people took reflected local squabbles, tensions and jealousies which had been in existence long before talk of war. When the war began many people wanted no part in it. Some formed inter-county neutrality pacts. In December 1642 the Royalist and Parliamentary gentry of Cheshire met together and agreed to disband all their troops. Quite often which side a group joined depended not on what they thought, but on which army arrived in their area first, forcing them to join that side. Later citizens set up groups of *clubmen* to defend their locality, by force if necessary, from the soldiers of either party. People changed sides, too, like Sir Edward Dering and Sir John Hotham.

In the end, however, two things probably played the major role in deciding which side people joined. One was religion – those who disliked what Archbishop Laud had been doing tended to join the Parliamentary ranks. The other was outlook – those who instinctively disliked change in religion, politics or society, generally sided with the king.

At the start of the war most advantages seemed to lie with the king. After all, he was the legitimate ruler, defending his rights, and those who opposed him were rebels. Royalist writers made this propaganda point time and again. The best example was in the king's answer to Parliament's Nineteen Propositions of 1642. He stood for security and peace, he claimed. He was foundation of all order. Overthrow the traditional ways, he argued, and the 'common people' would 'destroy all rights and properties, all distinctions of families . . . [so that] this splendid . . . form of government [would] end in a dark . . . chaos of confusion . . .' Arguments such as this were very effective at bringing men and women to the king's side. Charles also had the backing of the established church and the moral support of all foreign governments. His ranks contained more experienced soldiers than Parliament's. So why did he lose?

Parliament controlled the wealthier and more populous south and east of the country, giving it access to more manpower and money than the king. The navy, on which Charles had spent his

The Wounded Cavalier by the Victorian artist W.S. Burton. Before anaesthetics and proper medical treatment the gore and suffering of a battlefield was almost beyond belief. Which side do you think the painter shows most sympathy towards?

hard-won Ship Money, went over to his enemies at the outbreak of hostilities. This allowed Parliament to move men and supplies by sea and to intercept Royalist supplies from abroad. Although the Covenanter Scots were not always good soldiers, they were certainly more help to the Roundheads than were the Irish who helped the king in 1643.

There are many examples in history of poorer regions defeating richer ones. In the end it was not resources that gave Parliament victory. Rather, it was the use it made of those resources. The king's council of war was divided and his methods of raising money were inefficient. Parliamentary committees paid for the war by collecting an excise tax and regular weekly/monthly assessments and by seizing Royalist wealth. By these means they provided their armies with greater and more regular funds than the Royalists. This meant more regular pay, better armaments, better conditions for the men and so higher morale. At the last, this showed itself in a reorganized fighting force, the New Model Army. At Naseby this army finally put paid to any hopes of a Royalist victory.

CAVALIERS AND ROUNDHEADS

John Hutchinson makes up his mind

According to his wife, John Hutchinson thought long and hard before deciding which side to join in the Civil War.

> Mr Hutchinson . . . applied himself to understand the things then in dispute, and read all the public papers that came forth between the king and Parliament . . . Hereby he became . . . informed in his understanding, and convinced . . . of the righteousness of the Parliament's cause in . . . civil right; and though he . . . [believed the king was trying to undermine] the true protestant religion, yet did not think that so clear a ground for the war as the defence of . . . English liberties.
>
> (*Memoirs of the Life of Colonel Hutchinson*, written by his wife Lucy in the seventeenth century)

Anti-war feeling

In many parts of the country people's first reaction to the news that the king and parliament had taken up arms against each other was to declare themselves neutral. Later some areas made formal treaties of neutrality.

> An agreement made . . . at Bunbury, in the County of Chester, for a pacification and settling of the peace of that county . . .
>
> 1. It is agreed that there be an absolute cessation [stopping] of arms from henceforth within this county, and no arms be taken up to offend one another but by consent of the King and both Houses of Parliament, unless it be to resist forces brought into the county.
>
> (Cited in J. Morrill, *The revolt of the Provinces*, 1980)

Q

What was the crucial issue that made Hutchinson side with Parliament?

The younger children of Charles I and Henrietta Maria (with dates of birth, left to right): Mary (1631), Elizabeth (1635), James (1633), Henry (1639) and Henrietta Anne (1644).

CHECK YOUR UNDERSTANDING

Can you remember the meaning of the following:

aristocracy
clubmen
base
assessments
propaganda

THINGS TO DO

1 For Oliver Cromwell the English Civil War was ultimately about religion. There are several civil wars in the world today: find out what you can about them from television and newspapers and see whether religion plays any part in the conflict.

2 Using the pictures in this book, *Either*: Research the weapons used in the Civil War. Draw and label them, explaining their uses and the tasks in which they might prove most effective. *Or*: Look at the different clothes worn by Royalists and soldiers of the New Model Army – which do you think would be (a) the most comfortable to wear and (b) the best for fighting in?

A cartoon of Roundheads and Cavaliers with their dogs. Can you read what the dogs are saying and work out which side is which (look at the dog's hair!)?

A Loyal Cavalier

People took sides in the Civil War for all sorts of reasons. Sir Edmund Verney had little sympathy for the Church of England, but when war came he had no doubt about what he had to do.

> I do not like the quarrel, and do heartily wish that the king would consent to what ... [Parliament] desire; ... my conscience is only concerned in honour and gratitude to follow my master. I have eaten his bread and served him near thirty years, and will not do so base [mean] a thing as to forsake him.
>
> (From the autobiography of Charles I's advisor Edward Hyde, Earl of Clarendon)

Why, in the end, did Verney fight for the king?

The Issue at last

Unlike Hutchinson, for Oliver Cromwell the war was ultimately about religion.

> Religion was not the thing at first contested for, but God brought it to that issue at the last; and gave it unto us by way of redundancy [the only thing left]; and at last it proved that which was most dear to us.
>
> (Cited in Thomas Carlyle, ed., *The Letters and Speeches of Oliver Cromwell*, 1904)

Did everyone think religion was 'not the thing at first contested for'?

High taxes

Parliament's taxation enabled it to win the war, but it also aroused resentment.

> We are displeased that murmur at taxes ... whereat we should not quarrel, ... [because] we enjoy our lives, liberties, privileges, estates and religion ... [The king's taxes] were ... to ruin and enslave us ... these [Parliament's taxes] are to preserve us from it ...
>
> (John Bryan, *A Discovery of the Probable Sin*, 1647)

Do you think Bryan is honest in the way he uses the words 'we' and 'us'?

CAN YOU REMEMBER ?

At the start of the conflict which parts of the country did Parliament control? Which side did the navy fight on?

Who led the Scottish Covenanter army? Did people change sides in the Civil War?

THE ROAD TO WHITEHALL

When Sir Jacob Astley surrendered to the Roundheads at the close of the Civil War, he is supposed to have said to his captors, 'You have now done your work and may go play, unless you will fall out amongst yourselves.' It proved a most perceptive comment.

As we have seen, the Civil War was not fought between two clearly defined sides. When the fighting stopped in 1646, the situation was even more complicated than it had been in 1642. Some defeated Royalists wanted an agreement with Parliament, others believed there could be no compromise. The king himself seemed to hover between these two groups. Parliament was even more divided, not just about what sort of settlement to reach with the king, but also about the fate of the Church of England. Radical MPs (Independents) wanted tight limits on the king's powers and no official church. They thought each congregation should worship the way it wished. More moderate Parliamentarians looked for a slight reduction in the king's powers and a Presbyterian church (like Scotland's, without bishops and governed by a general assembly). Matters were not helped by the fact that Charles had surrendered to the Scots, who were themselves split into several factions. Finally, in England groups of extreme radicals had begun to spring up. These were the *Levellers*, who wanted drastic changes in England's society and politics to give everyone greater opportunities.

In 1646, as men and women reacted to years of high taxation, violence and disruption throughout the country, there was a feeling of general war-weariness. The New Model Army grew restless as its arrears (what was owing) of pay mounted. Parliament ordered the establishment of a Presbyterian church and offered Charles a settlement based on the Propositions of Newcastle in which he would not have to surrender too much authority. He refused to accept it. After negotiating with the Scots, Parliament eventually got control of the king in January 1647.

As often happens when normal forms of government break down, power passed into the hands of the army. Unpaid and discontented, the ordinary troops came under the influence of the London Levellers. When Presbyterian MPs reached an agreement with Charles and ordered the infantry to disband with only eight weeks' pay, the soldiers seized the king and occupied London. The Army was now a major political force. The trouble was that it was scarcely more united than the rest of the country. Two different sets of ideas for a way forward appeared. These were the officers' *Heads of the Proposals* and the Levellers' *Agreement of the People*. The two groups met at Putney in the autumn of 1647. Here they held long, inconclusive debates about what to do with the king and what sort of government the country ought to have.

Charles broke the deadlock. He escaped to the Isle of Wight and reached a settlement, known as 'the Engagement', with the Scots. Army officers broke off discussions, put down a Leveller mutiny in the ranks and went into action. During the Second Civil War (April–August 1648) the Army crushed a number of Royalist revolts and then, under the command of Oliver Cromwell, destroyed an army of

Scottish *Engagers* (those who had agreed to the Engagement with Charles) at Preston. Alarmed at the Army's growing power, some MPs re-opened negotiations with the king. On 6 December, perhaps on Cromwell's orders, Colonel Pride drove these MPs from the Commons. This action became known as 'Pride's Purge'.

As far as the leading army officers (the 'grandees') were concerned, the king's days were now numbered. As 'Charles Stuart that man of blood', he was blamed openly for the war. Those who opposed his execution argued that the majority of people did not want him killed, and it would only make him a martyr. But the grandees decided that as long as he lived there could be no settlement. They tried Charles before a special court. Although he denied its authority, it found him guilty. He was beheaded before a large crowd at Whitehall on 30 January 1649.

(Above) *Henrietta Maria, Charles' queen, friend and unflagging ally. Towards the end, however, even she began to tire of her husband's indecisive haggling with his captors.*

(Left) *The execution of Charles I at Whitehall on 30 January 1649 sent shivers of horror round all Europe.*

THE ROAD TO WHITEHALL

Radical new ideas

In the years between the ending of the Civil War and the execution of the king, for almost the first time in English history we can learn what ordinary people thought about the great issues of the day. One of the best sources is the 'Putney debates', when representatives of the rank-and-file soldiers spoke for the common folk. In this famous speech, Rainborough argues for all men to have a say in their government.

> For I really think that the poorest he [man] that is in England hath a life to live, as the greatest he; and therefore truly, sir, I think it's clear that every man that is to live under a government ought first by his own counsel [agreement] to put himself under that government . . .

(Cited in J. Kenyon, *The Stuart Constitution*, 1966)

Q

Why do you think the grandees were worried by remarks like this?

THINGS TO DO

1 Set out in your own words the arguments for and against executing Charles I.

2 *Either*: Imagine your family has supported Parliament throughout the Civil War. It is now autumn 1648. Write a letter to a friend explaining why you are worried at the way things appear to be turning out. *Or*: Imagine you are a common footsoldier in the New Model Army in the spring of 1648. Write a letter to your family explaining your hopes and fears for the future.

CHECK YOUR UNDERSTANDING

Can you remember the meaning of the following:

Independents
Presbyterians
Levellers
The Engagement

Royalists on the run

Once it was clear that Parliament had won the war, many Royalists fled abroad. Lady Ann Fanshawe remembered the hardship of her voyage from Cornwall.

> The next day, after having been pillaged, and extremely sick and big with child, I was set on shore almost dead in the Island of Scilly . . . I went immediately to bed, which was . . . vile . . . the whole house . . . consisted of four rooms, or rather partitions: two low rooms and two little lofts, with a ladder to go up. In one of these they kept dried fish . . . When I waked in the morning, I was so cold I knew not what to do, but the daylight . . . [showed] that my bed was near swimming with [in] the sea . . . With this we were destitute of clothes, and meat, and fuel, and truly we begged our daily bread of God, for we thought our every meal our last.

(From the *Memoirs* of Ann, Lady Fanshawe)

Q

Why do you think Lady Ann was so shocked at the state of the house she had to stay in?

Carisbroke Castle on the Isle of Wight, where Charles I was held after fleeing from the army. He had an opportunity to escape but refused to take it.

An End to Turmoil

In England the Second Civil War was partly an outbreak of popular discontent following years of high taxation, poor harvests and other misfortunes. This 1648 declaration from Dorset sums up the mood of many counties:

> We surviving inhabitants of the much . . . distressed County of Dorset having . . . long groaned under the oppressive tyranny . . . declare to the world what we mean to do for ourselves and the Kingdom.
>
> 1. We demand the speedy . . . [release] of our imprisoned King . . .
> 2. That the government of the Church may be . . . settled . . .
> 3. That the . . . Laws, may be restored to their former purity . . .
> 5. That we may have a speedy and just accompt [account] of all Monies and estates cheated or wrested [forced] from us by loans, contributions, taxes, fines, excise or plunder . . .

(Cited in J. Morrill, *The Revolt of the Provinces*, 1980)

'Such a groan'

A seventeen-year-old student witnesses the death of Charles.

> At the later end of the year 1648 I had leave to go to London to see my father, and during my stay there at that time at Whitehall it was that I saw the beheading of King Charles the First . . . On the day of his execution, which was Tuesday, January 30, I stood amongst the crowd in the street before Whitehall gate where the scaffold was erected, and saw what was done, but was not so near as to hear anything. The blow I saw given, and can truly say with a sad heart, at the instant whereof, I remember well, there was such a groan by the thousands then present as I never heard before and desire I may never hear again.

(An eyewitness account in the *Diary* of Philip Henry)

Bearing in mind which parts of the country were Royalist, do you think it significant that this declaration came from the south-western county of Dorset?

CAN YOU REMEMBER ?

Where did Charles I escape to?
Which settlement did Charles I refuse to accept in 1646?
Where did Cromwell defeat the Scots in 1648?

Why was Colonel Pride instructed to purge Parliament?
Who was known as 'that man of blood'?

THE RUMP

Oliver Cromwell forcibly dissolving the Rump, the remains of the Long Parliament which sat 1648–53. Like many Parliamentarians, Cromwell was fed up with waiting for the Rump to introduce useful reforms.

DIT HVYS IS TE HVER.

Be gone you rogues
You haue Sate long enough

C: Cuper

Parliament had won the Civil War and agreed to the setting up of a special court to try Charles I. And now that the king was dead, in theory Parliament was the supreme power in the land. But the Parliament of 1649 was not the same as that of 1642, or even that of 1645. It was smaller and more radical. Some MPs had died, many more had been thrown out in Pride's Purge. The remainder, nicknamed the Rump, were faced with the almost impossible task of trying to govern the country.

The nation was in turmoil. Radicals expected widespread reform of religion and society. Taking their inspiration from some of the more obscure parts of the Bible, some religious extremists believed the reign of King Jesus was about to begin on earth. Thousands of books, pamphlets and broadsheets poured from the presses, most demanding change. Ireland was still in chaos. On the Continent Charles II, the eldest son of Charles I, was looking for any opportunity to recapture the throne. Only days after Charles I's execution by the English, the Scots had proclaimed Charles II as their king. Almost all foreign powers were hostile to England's regicide regime (king-killing government). Finally, it was quite clear that

THIS HOVSE IS TO LETT

This is an Ivle.

was tightly censored and the more extreme religious groups were persecuted. Moderates were annoyed by some of the Puritan regulations, such as those abolishing Christmas and closing all theatres. But at least the Commonwealth survived, which, given the forces ranged against it, was no mean achievement.

In 1649 Cromwell crossed to Ireland with substantial forces of the New Model Army. His tactic for restoring English control was brutally simple. He besieged the Catholic strongholds at Drogheda and Wexford and ordered the merciless slaughter of their garrisons (September and October). Henceforward resistance crumbled. Cromwell returned to England in May 1650 and was made Lord General in June.

The following month Cromwell was on the move again, this time to Scotland where Charles II had landed and sworn to the Covenant. The Scots were defeated at Dunbar, and Edinburgh Castle fell to the English. But Charles II remained at large. He was crowned at Scone in January 1651 and in August he slipped past the English forces and marched south. It was a hopeless venture. In September Cromwell finally caught up with him at Worcester and destroyed his army, forcing him once more to flee into exile.

Scarcely was this danger over than the Rump found itself confronted with another. In 1651 it passed a Navigation Act to help English shipping against Dutch competition. Partly as a result of this, in May 1652 a naval war broke out between England and the United Provinces (Holland and the other Protestant parts of the Netherlands). Although the English fleet under Admiral Blake had some success, the expensive war was generally unpopular.

Suddenly, on 20 April 1653, Oliver Cromwell decided he had had enough of the Rump. Accompanied by soldiers, he entered the House and drove the MPs out. The Rump had not done what people wanted. It had not held elections, had carried out few reforms and had maintained a high level of taxation. Whatever his motives for dissolving it, Cromwell was in tune with the mood of the country. It was now up to him to see if he could do any better.

although in theory the Rump was running the country, in practice power still rested with the Army.

The Rump officially abolished the monarchy and the House of Lords and gave the task of day-to-day government to a Council of State. England was declared a Commonwealth, or republic. Many people were disappointed by the reforms that followed over the next three years. Compulsory church attendance was abolished, debtors were given some help and there were slight changes to the legal system, but little else. The press

The Escape of the king

After his defeat at Worcester in 1651, it was several weeks before Charles II escaped to France. His adventures, which included a day hiding in an oak tree, make an unforgettable adventure story.

From the 3 of September at Worcester to the 15 of October at Brighthelmston [Brighton] . . . he passed through more dangers than he travelled miles, of which . . . he traversed in that time . . . near three hundred . . . sometimes on foot with uneasy shoes; at other times on horseback . . . sometimes acting one disguise on coarse linen and a leather doublet [jacket] . . . one day he is forced to skulk in a barn . . . another day sits he with Colonel Carlos in a tree . . . and at night glad to lodge with William Penderel in a secret place . . . which never was intended for the dormitory of a king. . . . [T]hose rebels . . . so greedily sought his blood, yet by God's providence had not the power to discover him.

(Thomas Blount, *Boscobel*, a contemporary account of Charles' escape)

Mr Iane Lane and King:

the Kings escape in the sea Adventure.

The escape of Charles II after the Battle of Worcester. Can you pick out the battle, Charles hiding in a tree and disguised as a woman, and the ship which finally carried him to France from Shoreham?

Q

Why do you think many people were prepared to risk their lives to help Charles II escape?

CAN YOU REMEMBER ?

Where was Charles II crowned in 1651?
When did the Anglo-Dutch war begin?
Why was the Rump unpopular?
Why did Colonel Hutchinson knock down Nottingham Castle?
What two institutions were abolished shortly after the execution of Charles I?

(Left) *The Great Seal of the Commonwealth. Stamped on soft wax, this seal marked as official all documents to which the emblem was attached.*

CHECK YOUR UNDERSTANDING

Can you remember the meaning of the following:

Commonwealth
United Provinces
the Rump
Navigation Act
Regicide

A Righteous Judgement of God

The massacres at Drogheda and Wexford have never been forgotten, nor, by the Catholics, have they been forgiven. But to Cromwell himself the slaughter was doubly justified. Firstly, it was an effective way of discouraging further resistance. Secondly, he believed the Catholic Irish had slaughtered many Protestants during their rebellion. In his eyes, therefore, they were murderers who did not deserve humane treatment.

> ... in the heat of the action, I forbade them to spare any that were in arms in the town [Drogheda] ... I think, that night they put to the sword about 2,000 men ... about one hundred of them possessed St Peter's church-steeple ... These being summoned to yield to mercy, refused, whereupon I ordered the steeple ... to be fired, where one of them was heard to say in the midst of the flames: 'God damn me, God confound me: I burn, I burn.'
>
> ... When [others later] submitted, their officers were knocked on the head, and every tenth man of the soldiers killed, and the rest shipped for the Barbadoes [West Indies].
>
> I am persuaded that this is a righteous judgement of God upon these barbarous wretches, who have imbrued [stained] their hands with so much innocent blood ...
>
> (Cited in T. Carlyle, ed., *Letters and Speeches of Oliver Cromwell*, 1846)

Mistrust of Cromwell

Many who had fought for Parliament during the Civil War were alarmed at what happened after the execution of Charles I. Colonel Hutchinson, governor of Nottingham Castle, had hoped for liberty and reform. Instead, all he saw was Cromwell's growing power. He therefore did what he could to limit the Army's power.

> When the colonel heard how Cromwell used his troops, he was confirmed that he [Cromwell] and his associates in the army were ... [following their] private ambition ... Disdaining [rejecting], therefore, what he had preserved, for the liberty of his country ... in Cromwell's absence he procured [got] an order for the removal of the garrison at Nottingham [Castle] ... and for the demolishing of the place; which ... was speedily executed [done].
>
> (*Memoirs of the Life of Colonel Hutchinson*, written by his wife Lucy in the seventeenth century)

What 'private ambition' do you think Lucy Hutchinson is referring to?

Why did Cromwell consider the men he had slaughtered to have been 'barbarous wretches'?

THINGS TO DO

1 Find out more about Cromwell's behaviour at Drogheda and Wexford from the books in the reading list at the back, and give the arguments for and against his acting the way he did.

2 Suggest reasons why the Rump failed to win popular support.

3 Arrange a visit to one of the castles taken by the Roundheads in the war (see Finding Out More). Why do you think the occupants found it so difficult to defend themselves?

OLIVER CROMWELL

Oliver Cromwell dominated British history for much of the Interregnum. Few figures have been more controversial. His admirers praise him as a soldier of genius and as a tolerant and god-fearing political leader. They say he was genuinely concerned for the well-being of all people. He allowed religious toleration at home and his ability as a soldier was respected throughout Europe. Yet his critics condemn him as cruel and self-seeking, interested only in his own power. They say that if he had lived longer he would have become King Oliver I – the supreme betrayal of all he had fought for. His defenders claim that even if he had taken the crown (which was by no means a certainty), he would have done so to bring peace to the country, not for his own ambition.

It is impossible to sum up Cromwell neatly. He was a contrary and complicated man. Most things said about him, good and bad, are true, but none of them is the whole truth. Today, just as three hundred years ago, his genius cannot be captured in any one phrase.

From a prosperous East Anglian background, Cromwell first attracted attention as an MP opposed to the government in Charles I's third parliament (1628–9). After a long period of depression, during the 1630s he went through a religious conversion.

This left him convinced that he was one of God's chosen. He was now a puritan and an idealist, but a conservative in social matters. He sat in the Short and Long Parliaments, then made his name as a talented soldier with Parliament's Eastern Association. He was given command of the cavalry in the New Model Army and played crucial parts in Parliament's victories in the First and Second Civil Wars. In politics he swung between radicalism and conservatism, action and inaction, compromise and intolerance. The trial and execution of the king went ahead only when he had finally convinced himself that God wished it.

As commander-in-chief of the Army, Cromwell was away from London for much of the rule of the Rump. Once he had dismissed it, he had to take on the government of the country. His great problem, which he never solved, was how to change from military to civilian rule. He was never able to break free from the Army which had brought him to power.

First, he set up a Nominated Parliament or Parliament of Saints (sometimes also called the Barebones Parliament because of the odd name of one of its members). It was made up of 140 specially chosen religious Independents. Honest they might have been, but they were very inexperienced

(Left) *Oliver Cromwell, 1599–1658. Although probably the ablest Englishman of his generation, even he could not sort out the problems which the Civil War and execution of Charles I had thrown up.*

(Far left) *Cromwell after the Battle of Marston Moor. His brilliant command of the Parliamentary left had played a vital part in bringing victory in one of the crucial battles of the war.*

politicians and the experiment collapsed in December 1653. Cromwell now accepted a written constitution, the Instrument of Government, drawn up by the Council of Army Officers. This gave him widespread powers as Lord Protector but obliged him to call parliaments. These were filled with very independent-minded country gentry. He squabbled furiously with his first parliament and dismissed it as soon as he could. The second parliament fared little better and was dissolved in February 1658.

A Royalist rising in March 1655 gave Cromwell the idea of dividing the country into eleven districts, each controlled by one of his major-generals. Although unpopular and abolished by parliament, the scheme provided reasonably fair and effective local government for a time. In 1657 the constitution was altered by the Humble Petition and Advice. The Lord Protector refused the crown, but was given even greater powers, such as nominating his successor and setting up a new House of Lords –

the Other House. These changes alarmed both Royalists and Republicans.

Troubles at home were balanced by successes abroad. Cromwell ended the Dutch war, made favourable trade treaties with several countries and used the fleet to protect British merchants against Mediterranean pirates. In alliance with France, Britain went to war with Spain (1655). A West Indies expedition captured Jamaica and the reputation of the New Model Army spread to the Continent when an Anglo-French force defeated the Spanish in the Battle of the Dunes (June 1658).

However, no nearer establishing a lasting government to replace the one he had helped pull down, Cromwell died of pneumonia on 3 September 1658. He was buried at Westminster Abbey. Two years later following the restoration of Charles II his body was dug up and hung from the gallows at Tyburn.

Take away these baubles

Along with many of his contemporaries, Cromwell was disappointed at the Rump's failure to carry out widespread social and political reform. By using force to dismiss the Rump, Cromwell accepted the power of the army and ensured that henceforth the future of the country lay in his own hands.

> **The Lord General Cromwell came into the House [of Commons], clad in plain clothes, with grey worsted stockings, and sat down as he used to do in an ordinary place. After a while he rose up, put off his hat, and spake ... [Then] he changed his style, told ... [MPs] of their injustice, delays ... self-interest and other faults ... After this he said to Colonel Harrison: 'Call them in,' ... and presently [in came] five or six files of musketeers with their muskets ... Then the General went to the table where the mace lay ... and said, 'Take away these baubles.' So the soldiers took away the mace, and all the House went out ...**
>
> **(From a contemporary account in the *Sydney Papers*)**

On page 6 you can see a picture of Charles I in parliament. The figure in the bottom left corner is holding the mace – i.e. one of the 'baubles'.

The Great Seal of Oliver Cromwell. Compare it with the Great Seal of the Commonwealth on page 30.

For which 'delays' was Cromwell criticising the Rump?

CHECK YOUR UNDERSTANDING

Can you remember the meaning of the following:

Lord Protector
Barebones Parliament
Humble Petition and Advice
Instrument of Government
Eastern Association

THINGS TO DO

1 Compile a file on Oliver Cromwell. Draw up a chronology of his life, indicating its key turning points. List his strengths and weakness, his successes and his failures. Give his contemporaries' opinions about him and, at the end, sum up his life and achievements in your own words.
2 Imagine you are Oliver Cromwell in 1657. You are being urged to accept the crown. Decide what you will do and write a speech explaining your decision.

A brave, bad man?

These extracts show how divided Cromwell's contemporaries were in their opinions of the Lord Protector.

1. While admitting Cromwell to be a most able man, Lucy Hutchinson did not approve of what he did, nor of his hangers-on.

> Cromwell and his army grew wanton [careless] with their power, and invented a thousand tricks of government . . . First he calls a Parliament out of his own pocket [the Nominated Parliament] . . . Shortly after he makes up several sorts of mock Parliament, but not finding one of them absolutely to his turn, turned them off again. His wife and children were setting for principality [royalty], which suited no better . . . than scarlet on the ape; only, to speak the truth of himself, he had much natural greatness, and well became [suited] the place he has usurped [seized]. He at last exercised [used] such an arbitrary power, that the whole land grew weary of him, while he set up a company of silly, mean fellows, called major-generals . . . in every country.
>
> (*Memoirs of the Life of Colonel Hutchinson*, written by his wife Lucy in the seventeenth century)

2. Royalist James Heath believed Cromwell wanted nothing but the crown.

> From this haughty confidence he was invited to call another Parliament, and to assume . . . the long awaited result of his ambition, the Crown . . . of England.
>
> (*Flagellum: Or The Life and Death, Birth and Burial of Oliver Cromwell, the Late Usurper*, 1663)

3. Army chaplain Richard Baxter believed Cromwell was corrupted by power.

> . . . I think that, having been a prodigal in his youth and afterward changed to a zealous religiousness, he meant honestly in the main, and was pious and conscionable in the main course of his life till prosperity and success corrupted him . . .
>
> (*Reliquiae Baxterianae*, 1696)

4. Edward Hyde, later Earl of Clarendon, minister to both Charles I and his son, was more even-handed in his judgement.

> He was one of those men . . . (whom not even their enemies can curse unless it is to praise them at the same time); for he could never have done half that mischief (he was supposed to have done) without great parts of courage and industry and judgement. And he must have had a wonderful understanding in the natures and humours of men . . .
>
> He was not a man of blood . . . In a word, as he had all the wickedness . . . for which hell-fire is prepared, so he has some virtues which have caused the memory of some men in all ages to be celebrated; and he will be looked upon by posterity as a brave, bad man.
>
> (*History of the Rebellion*, 1702)

In extract 1, what criticism is Lucy making of Cromwell's family?

In extract 4, which of these judgements do you find the most convincing, and why?

CAN YOU REMEMBER ?

When did Oliver Cromwell die?
How many parliaments did he summon?
Which battle did the New Model Army fight on the
Continent?
What was Cromwell's title 1653–58?
Who helped with local government 1655–57?

RESTORATION

Just how important Oliver Cromwell had been in keeping the Republic together became clear shortly after his death. His 33-year-old son Richard became Lord Protector. He was a pleasant enough fellow, but had none of his father's political drive or talent. Nor, more importantly, did the Army think much of him.

The trouble came to a head when Richard's parliament met in January 1659. Conservative supporters of the Protectorate squabbled with Army-backed Republicans who wanted to return to the Commonwealth. In May the Army leaders forced Richard to dissolve parliament. The Rump was recalled and Richard resigned. This ended the Protectorate. Yet these moves solved nothing. The Rump immediately fell out with the Army, and the country began to slide into chaos.

Neither the Army nor the Rump had a clear idea of what they wanted. In such circumstances, all Charles II had to do was sit tight and wait until asked to return, which is precisely what he did. In

August the Army easily crushed Booth's Rising, a premature Royalist revolt in Cheshire. Two months later the Army drove out the Rump and ruled the country through a Committee of Safety. When it was clear that this was getting nowhere, the Rump was restored yet again.

At this point one of the key figures of the Restoration, General George Monck, made his appearance. From his base in Scotland Monck had watched the mounting chaos with dismay. Heeding calls for a 'full and free' parliament to sort matters out, early in 1660 he marched his army south and restored to the Rump all MPs excluded by Pride's Purge. In March 1660 the Long Parliament, which had first met in 1640, finally dissolved itself. Fresh elections were held for a convention parliament (one not summoned by a king). Then, from Breda in the United Provinces, Charles II issued a Declaration in which he set out the moderate terms under which he would return. Eager to get the whole business over with as swiftly as possible, on

The joyous scene as Charles II returns from exile. On his arrival, Charles made it his catch-phrase to 'never to go on his travels again'.

8 May the convention proclaimed Charles II to be the rightful king. Landing at Dover, the king reached London on 29 May. There was tumultuous rejoicing all over the country.

It may seem extraordinary that the restoration of the monarchy happened so suddenly and with so little violence. Part of the explanation is that the execution of Charles I had been the work of a small group of determined men, supported by the brute force of the Army. They had acted outside popular opinion and the republic they set up never won the hearts of the people. Also, by 1660 the once mighty Army was divided, and only Monck commanded an effective, disciplined force. The fear of anarchy (political chaos) was great. Economic distress added to the misery. Against this background the positive action of Monck and the moderation of Charles II made restoration almost a certainty.

The Restoration Settlement, put together between 1660 and 1665, began in a generous spirit. Charles was said to govern by divine right and was given a reasonable income to do so. The Act of Indemnity and Oblivion said that apart from those who had signed the death warrant of Charles I, there were to be no recriminations for what had happened over the previous twenty years. This mood of forgiveness did not extend to the religious settlement, which was put together by the Cavalier Parliament (1661–79). The Anglican church returned in all its glory. Those who refused to accept it were severely penalized in a series of acts known as the Clarendon Code. So much for the 'liberty to tender consciences' which Charles II had promised in the Declaration of Breda.

It is now clear that the Restoration had not really settled very much. There were still many questions unanswered. For example, the relationship between king and parliament (the great problem of 1640–2) was still not clear. It took a second revolution, in 1688, to sort the matter out properly (see the next chapter). For the time being, though, the conflict was over.

RESTORATION

Charles II

There can hardly have been two monarchs more different than Charles I and his son Charles II, nicknamed the 'Merry Monarch'. Bishop Burnet knew the young man well.

The King was then [1660] thirty years of age and, as might have been supposed, past the levities [silliness] of youth and the extravagance of pleasure. He had a very good understanding . . . He had a softness of temper that charmed all who came near him . . . He seemed to have no sense of religion . . .

He was affable [friendly] and easy, and loved to be made so by all about him . . . He had a great compass [extent] of knowledge, though he was never capable of much application or study . . . The ruin of his reign and of all his affairs was . . . [caused] chiefly by his delivering himself up at his first coming over [to England] to a mad range of pleasure.

(*A History of His Own Time*, Bishop Burnet, 1724–34)

Which of Charles' qualities mentioned above would have helped him heal the wounds of the Civil War and Interregnum?

The King enters London

In . . . magnificent fashion his majesty entered . . . the city of London at the bridge; where he found the windows and streets exceedingly thronged with people to behold him; and the walls adorned with hangings and carpets of tapestry and other costly stuff; and in many places sets of loud musick; all the conduits [pipes], as he passed, running claret wine; and the several companies in their liveries, with the ensigns belonging to them; as also the trained bands of the city standing along the streets as he passed, welcoming him with joyful acclamation.

(From a contemporary description in *Harleian Miscellany*)

Recalling the first year of the Civil War, what was ironic in the welcome of the city trained bands?

The capital welcomes the king: Charles II processing from the Tower of London to Westminster in 1661. It is said that a Cavalier living in Holland thought the news of the Restoration so funny that he died of laughter!

CAN YOU REMEMBER ?

Who succeeded Oliver Cromwell as Lord Protector? When did the Long Parliament finally dissolve? Who brought an army down from Scotland to restore order in England?

At the Restoration, which was the only group to be punished for what they had done between 1640 and 1660? What did Charles II give Ann Fanshawe's husband?

A King's Gratitude

In the end, after suffering the hardships of the Interregnum, all worked out well for Lady Ann Fanshawe.

The next day I went with the other ladies of the family to congratulate His Majesty's happy arrival, who received me with great grace, and promised me further favours to my husband and self. His Majesty gave my husband his picture, set with small diamonds, when he [the king] was a child: it is a great rarity, because there never was but one.

(From the *Memoirs* of Ann, Lady Fanshawe)

Why did Charles reward the Fanshawes?

Sad confusions in England

The diary of the puritan minister Ralph Josselin sums up well the confused feelings of many Parliamentarians as the republic collapsed. Later, although he refused to accept fully the new Anglican church, Josselin managed to keep his job.

25 January 1660 **This day I spent at Priory in a day of praise to my God . . . When I look back into the world I find nothing but confusions . . . sad wars in the north . . . and our poor England unsettled, and her physicians [i.e. politicians] leading her into deep waters. Cromwell's family cast down with scorn to the ground . . . the nation looking more to Charles Stuart, out of love to themselves not him, the end of these things God only knoweth; we have had sad confusions in England, the issue [result] God only knoweth.**

(From the *Diary of Ralph Josselin, 1616–1683*)

What did Josselin mean by saying that people were looking to Charles Stuart 'out of love to themselves not him'?

THINGS TO DO

1 Explain in your own words why Charles II was restored in 1660.
2 Imagine your are *either* a Royalist in exile *or* a foot soldier who had once fought for Oliver Cromwell. Write a long entry in your diary about the events of 1660.
3 Find other examples in world history where, after the overthrow of the government, power passed into the hands of the army.

CHECK YOUR UNDERSTANDING

Can you remember the meaning of the following:

Cavalier Parliament
'liberty to tender consciences'
Clarendon Code
Restoration Settlement

Why, after they had won the Civil War and got rid of the king, could the Parliamentarians not set up a government that lasted? One reason is that the Parliamentary side was made up of many, very different groups. The Royalists fought for their king because, in the last resort, they preferred things as they were to changes that might get out of control. The Parliamentarians, on the other hand, were in agreement only over what they did *not* want: arbitrary rule by the king, and a Church of England in the hands of Archbishop Laud. They did not agree on what they sought in their place.

Moderate Parliamentarians wanted the king to work more closely with parliament, an idea they put forward in the Propositions of Newcastle. The Levellers, such as John Lilburne, were at the other end of the scale. They wanted no monarchy, as little government as possible and a reformed parliament which reflected the wishes of most men.

The Parliamentarian's religious views were just as varied. The *Presbyterians* were among the more conservative. They hoped for a church without bishops, but set up by the government and covering the whole country. At times Charles I himself came close to accepting such an idea. The *Fifth Monarchists* were a good example of the most radical religious groups. Inspired by the more obscure parts of the Bible, they believed that the Fourth Monarchy (the Papacy) was about to collapse. When this happened, they believed, Jesus Christ would return to Earth to rule in person. Needless to say, to those who seriously believed this (such as Major-General Thomas Harrison) nothing else mattered. All they wanted was to get the Earth ready for this 'Godly reformation'. This meant wide-ranging social and religious changes. Although Cromwell had some sympathy with the religious hopes of such groups, he despised their extreme political views. As for the other radical groups, of the Levellers he was supposed to have once said: 'Break them, or they will break you'.

Given such a huge range of conflicting views among the Parliamentarians, it is hardly surprising that they failed to agree on a new constitution. The presence of the all-powerful Army made the situation still more complicated. Once it had become a political force, it was bound to influence what happened. Without the Army, Cromwell could not have come to power. But once in power, it was the Army which prevented him from taking the throne, although this was probably the only step which could have saved the new regime. The Army held the power to rule, but what it wanted was not necessarily what the country needed. In such a situation, a lasting settlement was almost impossible.

(Above left) *A sorry monument to civil war. Corfe Castle in Dorset, which Lady Bankes bravely held for the king from 1642 to 1646. Finally it was betrayed and ordered to be destroyed.*

(Right) *A rather fanciful picture of William III, the Dutchman who became King of England in 1689 after being invited to take the throne by parliament.*

Had the Civil War been fought for nothing? At first glance it might seem so. Less than two years after Cromwell's death, Charles II was on the throne, and Britain has remained a monarchy ever since. Many of the practical achievements of the years 1649–60 were lost. At the Restoration local government returned to the inefficient hands of the traditional rulers. Cromwell's unity of England, Scotland and Ireland, each sending MPs to a single parliament in London, was broken up. The religious toleration for most Protestants became a thing of the past.

But the clock could not be put right back. The laws of the Long Parliament that Charles I had signed remained in force. The new government took a leaf out of the Republican book and made sure that its policies helped the nation's merchants. But the most important legacy (remainder) of the Interregnum was neither a law nor a policy. It was an understanding. An understanding that kings and queens were there to serve the political nation, and if they did not do what was wanted, then they could be removed. This was not put to the test until 1688. In that year a second Stuart, James II, fell foul of the political nation. He was driven overseas, and his daughter Mary II and her husband William III were invited to reign in his place.

The 'Glorious Revolution' of 1688–9 was fixed in laws which finally showed that the nation had learned the painful lessons taught to the Cavaliers and Roundheads forty years before. In the end, therefore, perhaps the Civil War had not been entirely in vain.

Contrasting views

The range of views among those who sided against the king can be seen in these two extracts. The first is from the moderate Nineteen Propositions presented to Charles in June 1642. It says that parliament ought to deal with all important business. The king rejected the document, but before very long several of its suggestions had become part of the English constitution.

> 2. That the great affairs of the kingdom may not be concluded . . . by the advice of private men, or by any unknown . . . councillors . . . Such matters as concern the public . . . may be debated, resolved and transacted only in Parliament.
>
> **(Cited in J. Kenyon, *The Stuart Constitution*, 1966)**

The second extract is part of the programme of the Fifth Monarchists. They claimed that all earthly power came from Jesus. It was not to be wielded by parliament, but by a Supreme Council of Holy Men. All law was to be based on the Bible, and there was a long list of 'undesirable citizens' (such as the 'wicked bloody, Anti-Christian magistrates, ministers, lawyers' which it mentions).

> 1 . . . That all earthly governments, and worldly constitutions may be broken and removed by the . . . administration of the Kingdom of Christ . . .
>
> 6. That the supreme absolute [power to make laws] . . . is . . . in the Lord Jesus Christ . . .
>
> 7. That the scriptures . . . are the revealed will and rule of . . . [Christ], to be [followed] . . . in times of war and peace . . .
>
> iv. [The cost of war is to be born] . . . by those that are occasioners [starters] thereof, [e.g.] the beast and false prophet, the wicked bloody, Anti-Christian magistrates, ministers, lawyers etc . . .
>
> **(William Medley, *A Standard Set Up*, 1657)**

Q

Why do you think Parliament was afraid of 'private men'?
Why did many people not like the idea that the scriptures were the law?

Enamored of quietness

A political settlement was not the only legacy of the seventeenth century fighting. Englishmen and women, Cavaliers and Roundheads, learned to appreciate the ways of peace.

> What tumults we have seen and dangers past
> Such as in graves many thousand cast!
> And though I am no poet, I confess
> I am enamored [fond of] quietness.
>
> **(From a letter of Sir Aston Cockayne to Sir Henry Hastings, 1646)**

The Leveller John Lilburne, 1614–57, the radical of radicals, who was imprisoned by both Charles I and Oliver Cromwell for opposing their policies.

The Bill of Rights

The 1689 Bill of Rights, accepted by Queen Mary and King William, finally set out many of the rights for which parliaments, including Oliver Cromwell's, had been calling for almost fifty years. The Bill and the 1701 Act of Settlement marked the true conclusion to the struggles of Cavaliers and Roundheads.

4. That levying money for or to the use of the Crown . . . without grant of parliament . . . is illegal . . .

6. That the raising or keeping a standing army within the Kingdom in time of peace, unless it be with the consent of parliament, is against the law.

7. The election of members of parliament ought to be free . . .

13. And that for redress of all grievances [settlement of all complaints], and for the amending, strengthening, and preserving of the laws, parliaments ought to be held frequently.

(Cited John Wroughton, *Documents and Debates: Seventeenth Century Britain*, 1980)

CHECK YOUR UNDERSTANDING

Can you remember the meaning of the following:

Bill of Rights
Glorious revolution
Fifth Monarchists
redress of grievances

Major-General John Lambert, 1619–84, one of Cromwell's ablest and most ambitious commanders. He was no politician, however, and in 1658–9 failed to read the mood of the nation. As a result he spent the last 22 years of his life imprisoned in various isolated fortresses.

CAN YOU REMEMBER ?

Who was driven off the throne in 1688?
Why was there no lasting settlement during the Interregnum?
Which set of proposals did Parliament give to Charles I in June 1642?
Whom did the Fifth Monarchists believe was the Supreme Lawgiver?
MPs from which nations met in Cromwell's Parliaments?

Why do you think clause 4 did more than clause 13 to ensure frequent parliaments?

THINGS TO DO

From what you have read in this book, compare religion's importance in everyday life in seventeenth century England and today.

What Can You Remember?

What was the family name of James I, Charles I, Charles II and James II?

What two names may be given to the period 1629–40?

Who was Charles I Archbishop of Canterbury for most of the 1630s?

In which country did military opposition to Charles I begin?

What was the first major battle of the English Civil War?

How many people died as a result of the Civil Wars?

What was the name of Parliament's reorganized army of 1645?

Why was the battle of Preston fought?

When was Charles I executed?

What is the comic name given to Cromwell's first Parliament?

What happened at Drogheda?

Who were the Fifth Monarchists?

Why did Cromwell not accept the crown?

Which West Indian island did Cromwell's forces capture?

When was Charles II restored?

TIME CHART

1625	Accession of Charles I
	Charles collects customs without parliament's approval
1626	King raises forced loans
1628	House of Commons draws up Petition of Right
	Duke of Buckingham assassinated
1629	Beginning of Personal Rule (to 1640)
1632	Wentworth becomes Lord Deputy in Ireland
1633	Laud becomes Archbishop of Canterbury
1634	Charles raises Ship Money for the first time
1637	New Prayer Book imposed on Scotland – riot and rebellion
1638	Scots form National Covenant
1639	First Bishops' War
	Taxpayers strike in England
1640	Short Parliament
	Second Bishops' War – Treaty of Ripon
	Long Parliament (on and off to 1660)
1641	Act preventing dissolution of Long Parliament without its own consent
	Execution of Strafford
	'Incident' in Scotland
	Irish rebellion
	Grand Remonstrance
1642	King fails to arrest five MPs and leaves London
	Battle of Edgehill
	King turned back at Turnham Green
1643	First Battle of Newbury
	Solemn League and Covenant between Parliament and Scots
1644	Battle of Marston Moor
1645	Laud executed
	New Model Army set up
	Battle of Naseby
1646	Charles I surrenders to Scots
	Newcastle Propositions given to Charles I
	Parliament sets up a Presbyterian church

1647	Charles I handed over to Parliament, then seized by Army
	Putney Debates
	Charles I escapes and signs Engagement with Scots
1648	Second Civil War
	Battle of Preston
	Pride's Purge of Long Parliament
1649	Trial and execution of Charles I
	Charles II proclaimed in Edinburgh
	Monarchy and House of Lords abolished; England a Commonwealth
	Slaughter of Catholic Irish at Drogheda and Wexford
1650	Charles II to Scotland
	Battle of Dunbar
1651	Battle of Worcester and flight of Charles II
	Navigation Act
1652	Anglo-Dutch War (to 1654)
1653	Cromwell expels Rump
	Barebones Parliament
	Instrument of Government, Cromwell Lord Protector
1654	Treaties with United Provinces, Sweden, Portugal and Denmark
1655	Penruddock's Royalist rising
	Rule of major-generals (to 1657)
	War with Spain; capture of Jamaica
1657	Humble Petition and Advice; Cromwell rejects crown
1658	Death of Oliver Cromwell; Richard Cromwell Lord Protector
1659	Richard Cromwell resigns
	Rump recalled
	Booth's rising
1660	General Monck marches south
	Convention parliament
	Declaration of Breda
	Restoration of Charles II
1688	Flight of James II; Glorious Revolution (to 1701)

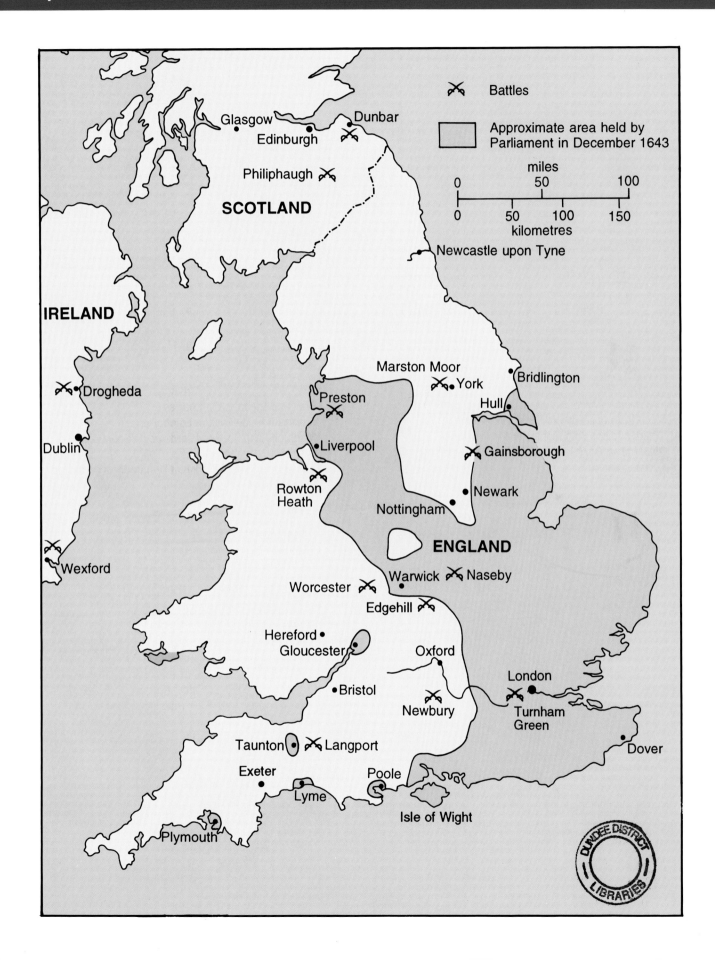

Battles

Approximate area held by Parliament in December 1643

miles
0   50   100
0   50   100   150
kilometres

Glasgow
Edinburgh
Dunbar
Philiphaugh
SCOTLAND

Newcastle upon Tyne

IRELAND

Drogheda

Dublin

Wexford

Marston Moor
York
Bridlington
Preston
Hull
Liverpool
Gainsborough
Rowton Heath
Newark
Nottingham

ENGLAND

Warwick
Naseby

Worcester
Edgehill

Hereford
Gloucester
Oxford
London
Turnham Green

Bristol
Newbury

Taunton
Langport

Exeter
Poole
Dover
Lyme
Isle of Wight

Plymouth

DUNDEE DISTRICT LIBRARIES

GLOSSARY

Anglican   relating to the Church of England

aristocracy   the noble upper classes

Arminianism   Protestant belief based on the ideas of Jacobus Arminius

Barebones Parliament   Cromwell's first Parliament, sometimes named after one of its lesser-known members (see also Nominated Parliament)

Bill   a proposed new law

broadsheet   a printed news sheet

canon   church pronouncement

Cavalier   nickname for a Royalist

Cavalier Parliament   first parliament of reign of Charles II, sat 1661–79

Clarendon Code   legislation 1661–65 taking away most rights from non-Anglicans

Commonwealth   England and its constitution 1649–53

compromise   an agreement favouring no particular side

constitution   laws and customs by which a country is governed

convention   Parliament not summoned by a monarch

coup   to take over the government by force

Covenant   religious-nationalist agreement adopted by the Scots opposed to Charles I and his church

Declaration of Breda   declaration in which the exiled Charles II set out the terms of his return to the English throne

dissolve   disband or get rid of

Divine Right of Kings   belief that kings were appointed by God and answerable to Him alone

Dragoon   heavily armed, mounted soldier

Engagement   agreement between Charles I and some Scots, 1647

excise   tax raised on the sale of goods

gentry   the upper-middle classes

Glorious Revolution   the overthrow of James II in 1688 and the legislation which followed, 1689–1701

Grandees   leading officers of the New Model Army

Humble Petition and Advice   revised constitution offered to Oliver Cromwell, 1657

Independents   those rejecting any form of national church

Instrument of Government   constitution accepted by Oliver Cromwell in 1653

Interregnum   period between reigns of Charles I and Charles II, 1649–60

Kirk   the Scottish Church

Levellers   those who wished for a radically more equal society

Long Parliament   parliament which sat, on and off, 1640–59

Lord Protector   title adopted by Oliver and Richard Cromwell, 1653–59

Nominated Parliament   Cromwell's first Parliament, filled with MPs selected for their virtue and holiness (see Barebones Parliament)

peer   noble

political nation   those with political power and influence

popery   slang term for Roman Catholicism

prerogative   royal authority

Presbyterianism   form of Protestantism in which authority rested with congregations and a church assembly, not with king or bishops

Pride's Purge   Colonel Pride's removal of MPs who had sought agreement with Charles I, which took place in 1648

propaganda   information designed to give a particular point of view

Protectorate   government by Lord Protector

puritan   'hotter sort of Protestants' who wished to see all remnants of Roman Catholicism (usually including bishops) removed from the church

radical   in favour of fundamental change

regicide   the killing of the king

remonstrance   complaint

republic   country governed without a monarch

Restoration   the return of Charles II to the throne, 1660

revolution   change that is complete, fundamental and usually swift

Roundheads   slang name for the Parliamentarians

Rump   Long Parliament MPs who survived Pride's Purge

Sabbath   Sunday, or the Lord's Day

scaffold   platform for executions

Ship Money   tax collected to pay for the upkeep of the Royal Navy

47

Short Parliament   Parliament which sat April–May 1640
statute   Parliamentary law
trained band   locally-raised part-time force of soldiers

United Provinces   Holland and the other Protestant states of the Netherlands
writ   official document confirming or demanding something

FINDING OUT MORE

For younger readers

A. Clarke, *Growing Up in Puritan Times*, 1980
A. Dures, *How and Why: the English Civil War*, 1987
L. Mendes, *The English Civil War*, 1982
H. Pluckrose, *Stuart Britain*, 1981
S. Ross, *Spotlight on the Stewarts*, 1987
J. Saraga, *Cromwell*, 1990
S. White-Thomson, *Oliver Cromwell and the Civil War*, 1984

For older readers

G.E. Aylmer, *Rebellion or Revolution?*, 1986
T. Barnard, *The English Republic, 1649–1660*, 1982
C. Carlton, *Charles I*, 1981
B. Coward, *The Stuart Age*, 1978
C.W. Daniels and J. Morrill, *Charles I*, 1988
D. Hirst, *Authority and Conflict*, 1986
A. Hughes, *Seventeenth-Century England: a Changing Culture*, 1980
J.P. Kenyon, *The Civil Wars in England*, 1987
          , *The Stuart Constitution*, 1986
J. Morrill, *The revolt of the Provinces*, 1980
          , *The Impact of the English Civil War*, 1991
I. Roots, *The Great Rebellion 1642–1660*, 1979
C. Russell, *The Causes of the English Civil War*, 1990
          , ed., *The Origins of the English Civil War*, 1973
K. Wrightson, *English Society 1580–1690*, 1982

Acknowledgements

The Author and Publishers would like to thank the following for their permission to reproduce illustrations: Ashmoleum Museum for pages 6, 8/9; Ronald Sheriden Ancient Art and Architecture Collection for page 22; Bridgeman Art Library for pages 1, 5 (left and right), 9, 20, 21, 24/25, 25 (top), 27, 32, 33, 36/37, 40; British Library for page 19; British Museum for page 34; e.t. archive for pages 16, 17; Mansell Collection for pages 18, 24/25, 43; National Portrait Gallery for pages 4, 15, 22, 42; and to Ken Smith for drawing the map on page 45.

Thanks go to the *How It Was* series editors for advice and editorial input: Jessica Saraga, Madeline Jones and Michael Rawcliffe.

Places to visit

There are many smaller local museums with exhibits from the Civil War era, but the following sites and museums are especially worth a visit: Boscobel (Shropshire), Broughton Castle, Chastleton House (Oxfordshire), Banqueting House (Whitehall, London), Corfe Castle (Dorset), Dunnotar Castle (Grampian), Colleges at Oxford, Earthworks at Newark (Nottinghamshire), Barbican at Plymouth (Devon), Compton Wynyates House (Warwickshire), Hillesden House (Buckinghamshire), and Warwick Castle (Warwickshire).

INDEX